LANDSCAPES
and LEGACIES

Landscapes
and
Legacies

Tom Pow

ι υ γ ξ

iynx publishing

First Published by

iynx publishing
Countess of Moray's House
Sands Place
Aberdour
Fife
KY3 0SZ

A CIP catalogue record for this book is available from the British Library

ISBN 0-9540583-4-8

The Publisher acknowledges subsidy from the

Scottish
Arts Council
towards the publication of this volume

Typeset by Edderston Book Design, Peebles
Printed and bound in Great Britain by Creative Print and Design, Ebbw Vale

Aim in life –
Oh to cover my shame with regal attire!

Czeslaw Milosz

CONTENTS

Some of these poems have appeared in the following –

Stand, Northwords, Markings, The Dark Horse, Carapace (S.A.), The Scotsman, Chapman, Cencrastus, Lines Review, Poetry Scotland.

Anthologies: *Poems from Scotland* (Macmillan), *New Writing Scotland* 15, 16, 17 (ASLS), *New Writing 10* (Picador), *Love for Love* (Pocketbooks/Polygon). The fifth of the *Legacies* sequence first appeared in *Red Letter Day* (Bloodaxe).

Landscapes, with linocuts by Hugh Bryden, was published by Cacafuego Press in a limited edition. A framed edition of the book was part of a touring exhibition, *Pagemakers*, organised by Dumfries and Galloway Council.

I would like to acknowledge the support of the Scottish Arts Council in the course of writing this book. The final deliberations for it were made during a Hawthornden International Fellowship. Many of these poems have grown from the generosity of people prepared to share their landscapes with me. I am most grateful to them all.

For different reasons, relating to this present work, I would also like to thank Stewart Conn, Robyn Marsack and Diana Hendry.

In *Danube*, Claudio Magris comments on the tension and opposition there can be between 'the family from which one comes . . . and the family which one founds.' The first is part of 'the world of unalterable things' our relationship to which it takes a lifetime to understand; while 'the other family, the family which one brings into being, is an arduous and unpredictable odyssey full of pitfalls and temptations, sunsets and new dawns.'

I would like to substitute 'joyful' for 'arduous' in Magris' quote and dedicate this book to both my families.

Section One

Hoboes

Hoboes

Europe, Between Wars

I got stones in my passageway
and my road is dark as night
Robert Johnson

I

Brother, here lives a kind woman –

Chance brought me to her door.
She took me in without question
filthy as I was. How long

had I been dancing? Hard to tell.
I came to myself, yelping like a dog
round a sycamore. She called me

from the shadows, her cats' milk
dripping from my chin. Cats,
the kindest keep them. She'd two,

black as night. They wove
between her ankles; they came
to me as she bathed and bound

my bleeding feet. Kindness, hatred –
who's closer to the Mysteries
than we are? – the look of one, the brush

of the other. She lived alone
with an orphaned busy-ness
even my needs couldn't touch.

I saw her eyes, in passing, kiss
the mantel portrait of a waxen soldier
more than once. I took to the barn

with a blanket from her bed,
bread and cheese from her table.
Through a crack in the wood

I saw the moon – the first time
in a long time – as a possible friend.
And that night, I swam without pause

from one empty room to another.
I woke with a knocking at her door,
then the rough, insistent voices.

II

Brother, you should have heard me!

At first, I gleaned our old familiar,
Suspicion, from her eyes. It was
the children brought me to her –

I'd taught them pick-up-sticks
in the lane. *Wait there* – they'd bring me
tea with sugar, milk; bread and jam.

All the while, their bright eyes flitted
between us. Look! – we've brought
a maimed bird to your door.

There were three of them, lithe
as cats, and briefly trusting too.
As one handed me the bread

I told how happy I'd been up north:
good job . . . lovely wife . . . O every
possible blessing, till a story

of sudden betrayal lifted me
out of my life, clear of
the growing of my children, to live

on the road, keeping secret shrines,
a guardian of only my own ageing.
It was a toss up: that one

or the Jesus story, and I chose well
for without further word she brought
thick slices of pork, a blanket

of good grey wool. Yet even
in triumph, wreathed in her smile,
I couldn't shake the loss of what

I'd never had. Brother, beware
the power of your own persuasions.
                                        At times
better an empty belly, the open road.

III

Brother, when she laid eyes on me,

she called him double quick; the pair of them
side by side, filling out the doorway.
Whatever they said, I had their meaning.

What do you want?
You can't stay here. You must leave.
Leave now. Their eyes, jittery

as caged birds, scanned the horizon:
what lay beyond the roads that brought me
to their door? 'We're good people,'

she told me, thumbs buried in her fists. 'But . . .'
I stood – call this the Third Art –
letting her words fall into silence.

A child poked a blunt head round her legs.
I smiled at the child. 'Please,' its mother said.
Brother, the first two arts will save your bacon,

but only if you're quick. The Third Art
is to trust in stillness. St Francis
had it in spades. All other holy men too.

In the end, she'd no answer
to whatever brought the thumping
to her chest. Round the back,

sun on a sweet smelling wood stack,
he slopped milk into my tin mug;
she pushed at me half a loaf of fruit bread.

'Now,' he said, near to being friendly,
'head for the birch wood. It's dense. I work
the fields close by. More of your kind's

hiding out in there. I've heard pipes,
seen the shadows dancing.'
His 'good luck' barely reached my back.

I took it for someone else's prayer.

IV

Brother, this is a good place to be.

The couple are old, the house
and the dogs sleep early. Time then
to leave the barn, *To walk out*

of an evening. My advice, head
for the orchard; even in clearest
moonlight, its trees will hide you.

You'll stroll between their slim
and eager young branches, plucking
an apple here, a plum or two there.

It's like living in the strange land
of Plenty. You may choose to eat
as you pick; at other times

collect a lapful of fruit
and lie against a tree, breathing in
the rising sweetness. How can you

know anticipation when you
have nothing? It's only
to invite a fanged beast to your door.

But now, the fruit
gathered, let the moment last
as long as you want it to. This

is the beginning of things again –
a church of earth and of air. Let
the darkening world beyond

this sleepy farm fend for itself –
moonlight and fruit are yours.
But brother, don't stay too long,

be careful where you pick –
a pattern of bark-wounds
can be read clear as any book.

Contained appetites are better
for those who return; those
lucky enough to come after.

V

Brother, didn't you read the signs?

This is no place to linger. Once
we were shadows, seasonal as plants.
But, though their eyes kept us

at the furthest rim of vision, crouching
in half light over our tidy fires,
not much missed us

of the silhouettes that fought
or danced in lamplight; we heard
the kicked dog yelp, the low moan

of the rotten-hoofed beast;
the snagged sheep calling out
to an indifferent flock.

Of course when she was found,
on a bed of crushed anemones,
her white chest naked as a swan's,

they preferred to think evil
had been imported: that the theft
of a few hen's eggs or a slack udder

were preludes to such a cruelty.
He laid her down, the cord beside her,
and scrabbled around in wood litter.

He glanced my way, then
sniffed the air. I tell you he knew
someone was watching. But what's

our word worth? Stay –
they'll get us both for something.
Over the border, so I've been told's

a safe place to camp and fresh water.
See that broken old stump on the skyline?
From there, you're on your own.

VI

Sister? I've heard the stories too –

the clear shape of you curled
in morning mist, cut
from the evenings' shadows. What was it

18

drove you onto the road, to live like this —
no home, no love, only these coded
messages, these random notes to ourselves?

It's said, most often, you pass
as a man with a heavy coat,
a scarf, worn like a cowl, nodding

resolutely as if no force
could face you. But beneath the coat,
so say those who've caught you

in river or lake, the uncoiled nest
of hair a shadow-you swimming
beside you, your nakedness

is only one of many signs. Is it
you then that unites us? You
who moves between us in our

orphanhood, making us feel —
who are careful to feel — we may not be
so completely alone. Sister —

when I pass by a blue shrine
I imagine it is you. When I am a dog
burrowing in the damp earth, I smell

the first effulgence of spring
and imagine it is you. When I feel
the slight wind on my brow at night

I imagine your fingers, your lips,
passing onto me the sweetness
of a mother, a lover, a daughter, a wife.

VII

Brother, there are times in sleep

I'm in a world that's fresh
with new signs; birds I feel
I know yet can't quite name.

I'm at home there, sunning myself
on top of a freight car beneath a sky
that scrolls out blue and blue

and blue over an endless prairie.
By the time I reach one coast
I'm forgotten at the other. I pass

over the earth just once. At times
I meet others of my kind – men
and women rich in stories. We fish a river,

fiercely blue as the sky; cook trout
over an open fire, sing sad songs
we wouldn't have any other way.

I got stones in my passageway
and my road is dark as night.
It is better is it not than living

in this world of black and white,
cleaving to a rail track as thick smoke
shrouds us where we crouch

in the shadows? When I go round
the doors with my clothes pegs
or a basket of whittled dolls

I've to get a story out quick –
and a strong one too! – or I'm fucked
by a fable I can't escape. In their dreams

I'm bound in black rags: some kind
of carrion poisoning water wells,
picking over their dead.

VIII

Brother, how I got here's a mystery:

sleeves like washing on a line
drew me; washing that moved
to a musical line, say the droned

exhalation of a bagpipe. The shirts hung
from a hand cart or a trailer;
and a straggle of men followed

after the cart, singing softly
as if to themselves,
'More light! More light!'

The shirts were for hire –
woollen they were, the colour
of straw. We wore them loose

over our clothes and tied
a thick worsted tie round our necks
like a noose. So dressed

we followed the trailer or cart
and smiled on our fellow men
as we shuffled along like pilgrims –

yes, pilgrims is what we seemed to be.
And though the light was strong,
and stronger yet as the day wore on,

still we sang, 'More light! More light!'
It wasn't a musical – it felt so real!
And if it was a dream,

then other bloods had lived it.
As our shirts bathed in the burning
fields of light, it was unclear

whether we were celebrating
or mourning; chanting in elegy
for the darkness we were leaving

or in praise of the open road ahead.

Section Two

Landscapes

Crabs: Tiree

We tied a worm of bacon fat
to a flat rock with string
and dropped it over the edge
into the clear water
of the bay. It fell gently

to the sand and the seaweed.
A tug told us we'd a bite
or we saw the crab itself
latch onto the ragged fat and pulled it
steadily out: this was the knack.

Too sudden, too sharp
and it dropped from its stone
shadow, so clumsily evading
its fate. But smoothly
feeding the rough string

through fist upon fist
and they would come to us
like lumps of lava, water
sluicing from their backs.
Dumbly determined

they hung on
by one improbable claw
before the dull crack as they hit
the harbour wall or the side
of the pails we kept them in.

Standing in a row
four or five of us holiday kids
pulled out scores in a day till each
bucket was a brackish mass
of fearsome crockery

bubbling below
its skin of salt water.
What happened to them all? –
our train of buckets, the great stench
of our summer sport.

It was a blond boy
from Glasgow finally pushed me in
head over heels from where
I crouched on the pier wall.
When I righted myself

I was waist deep in crab–
infested waters. No one
could pull me out. 'You must walk
to the shore,' my sister shouted
as I held my hands

high above my head
thinking I could at least
save them. But how beautiful
it was all around me! The spatter
of green crofts

and deep blue lochans,
the cottontail, the buttercup
on the cropped foreshore. The sky
was depthless; all was silence.
And I was there

moving slowly through
this perfect blue wedge
bearing terror in one hand, guilt
in the other, leaving the briefest wake
to mark my shame.

Mr McArthur

The rogue sheep on its knees nudges
a bony head at the kettle
of milk on my lap. I hold both
handle and lid with canny conceit,
for the kettle's tin sides
are in the broad grip of our host,
Mr McArthur himself, whose arm
brushes my cheek with sweet
smells of straw and milk.
                              Each evening
he places the white jug of milk
straight from the cow beside butter
and jam. And for a moment
stands in the door, a large-boned, florid
featured man whose bottom teeth jut
over toothless gums. Our mother smiles
with a 'That-will-be-fine-thank-you,'
and a shoulder-straightening that says
No childish words please – on the still
steaming milk, its surface jewelled
with golden gobs of fat.
                              The oiled coat
of the sheep brushes my knees
and I curl my fingers away
from the desperate milk-whiskered mouth.
What a useless little bugger
I am! Seven years old I let slip
two faded floral cups, then
watch Mr McArthur bearing
the pieces away like petals
in his raw hands. A gate's spar cracks
when I swing on it; a door's slat –
I swear – caves in before the wind.
But Mr McArthur simply
smiles or tuts as if nothing
is worth anything – or as if
the landscape of wind, rain and sea

is too fluid for the tight space
of apology we'd pen him in.

Saying goodbye in that boxed hall
with the new-mended door, I sense
the generous presence of his life;
the routine acts he's opened up
to me. How have I repaid him?
We have no language but this
clumsy disclosing of ourselves.
My tears are black on the stone flags.
I know they are no apology –
but in the stiff silence *sorry*'s
not what I want to say most.

Clestrain: Orkney

Boyhood home of John Rae –
Arctic Explorer.

On a cloud-stacked spring afternoon
you can hear how even the mildest wind
buffets your voice into a mourn-
ful staccato, how words are thinned

down to their roots. Yet his voice
rasped through the elements, on the edge
of each curt order, a savage
delight in hardship. At the *noust* –

the cleft of rock where his sailboat
was once snug – I turn from the shore
and, cleaving to a dyke for shelter,
take the track to the sensibly squat

house of Clestrain. Here the wind's cut
and the stones tell only of absence,
broken by a last pigeon caught
fluttering out one more vacant lens.

There's a skeleton grandeur still –
the curled ironwork that lurches
from the staircase – a dainty school
indeed for the man who marched

till his moccasins were blood-shod;
who made soup from rotting fish-bones
and claimed you knew nothing of food
till you'd drained the last juices down

from a ptarmigan's toes. The thoughts
spool on, with a creak from a board,
a scuffed stone; a vision that rots
in the silence: the place can't hoard

the man. Out in the minch, a boy
hauls on a flapping sail, careless
of weather. Rain shushes like a sleigh;
flinty waves strain in their tresses.

But the boy looks past the cloth he holds
to the horizon's sudden silver:
beyond which lies death — or adventure —
and over which the stories roll.

An African Childhood

Blantyre, Malawi, 1997

In the late afternoon,
Papa announced a walk before dinner,
    and we took off – Cecily
on her small push-bike, Papa striding out

    in shorts, his walking stick
pointing the way, clearing the air before us,
    drawing diagrams in dust.
In bursts, I raced Papa along avenues

    of jacaranda, past cool
bungalows wrapped by fences, freighted
    with the most dire warnings.
And always Papa talked – the way he walked –

    in that clipped, decisive way,
the precision of the not-quite native speaker.
    He told us the palace grounds,
through which we passed along an unkempt path,

    were once thought sacred; though now
the valley was stripped of timber, its dry earth
    ribbed by hand ploughs.
Voracious, a word that came later, best

    described Papa, with his
appetite for learning, for languages,
    for mending all manner
of things – which, he made clear, a doctor here

    had to be able to do.
But, as the pure African light dims
    and the crimson sun brushes
the rim of distant hills, we must quicken

our pace; now my chasing legs
have deserted me; now Cecily's face
   shines and pinches with effort.
When we come to the Township, we wind our way

   through and past all the locals
out on *passageo*, in what I see now
   as the life of a musical.
Such colour! Such theatrical density!

   Children groomed on stoops;
men swilling beer in dark, rush-roofed bars;
   bed-life, night-life – the blurred
movements of unfenced lives. And, as the light

   grows grainier still, we take
a shortcut, always trusting Papa, up
   fetid alleys, clamped between
shacklike homes, along overgrown tracks

   with the piquant, hothouse smells
of rotting vegetation – fearful of snakes –
   and it's all uphill now!
Till suddenly we spill out onto

   the familiar red road.
We slip into our house the back way, past
   the quiet servants' quarters,
through the yard, the lightly tapping screen,

   just as Mama's wondering
where Papa may have led us. Already,
   as I feel my bare feet cool
on the floor, night's snatched the landscape

   back from us – and Papa's
standing at the sink, unchanged, leaning over
   a recipe, gutting a pile
of silver fish for a supper *bouillabaise*.

Alabama

(Sequence of photographs by Walker Evans)

In the first of the sequence, top left,
there's a corner of leaves like congealed
light. Evans crops them, his camera
clipping the top of the father's hat
till there's nothing of natural beauty
suggested here, if it's not a fragile

choreography – the echoing
elegance of gesture, the rhombus
of arms lifting hair from a damp neck,
the tilt of a man's head, as he draws smoke
through the parched air. For richer
or poorer, an image of family.

Evans takes us down, down to the dust
of the earth. Look! it's to handfuls of dust,
not to light, we're all headed. Down
to the crook of wall and stoop, where a patched
mongrel pants away the day. Down
to bare feet, rough as tools, as planks –

planks on the stoop, their ends like ragged nails.
Down to the chancy boulder stones, perched
precariously one on the other,
which hold for now the weight of family.
But if you advance too far on the stoop,
like the youngest, you'll be screwing up

your eyes against the light – the light
which even in shadow holds the deep folds
of their sack-like shifts, the watchful faces
of children, the lean planes of the face
of the father. It's mostly where they live,
out here, between darkness and light.

For through the window, through the doorway,
darkness waits for them to entrust one more
small part of themselves into its care.
There's a simple wooden table there,
with little, God knows, to put on it,
but each evening laden with prayers.

Strawberries

The Algonquins, Canada

In the middle of a landscape
that could lose us – one small boat
and a sun jig-sawing away
great bays of black waters to give

one last rhythmic shape of light –
Rosa's hand uncups a harvest
of wild strawberries she's gathered
on the lake's shore. In muted light,

each red fleck glows: a tiny coal,
the whole a brazier of strawberries,
which calls from us all something brief
but shared – delight or prayer –

before we press out their sweetness
with our tongues. A dragonfly
comes at us now from far along
its steady thread of flight. In fact,

we're losing detail fast – the lake's
brimming to a darkening crush
of firs, appears to be a step higher
than us. This boat's heading

for the impossible, I think,
as one heron, then another,
heave themselves from the shadows and,
trailing the grainy daylight, take

all the time two blue herons need
to sew darkness onto darkness
across the bay. Any time now,
the riper stars will start to glow.

By the time we're barbecuing
back at base, our hungry eyes'll
scoop them up like beer nuts, rootless
and rife in every patch of sky.

The Gift

from Andy Goldsworthy

I thought, given they were small
as children's fists, the pigeons' breasts
would cook quickly. But my wife

found them too rare. She pointed out
at the end of one clean pink slit
the bloody hole the shot had made.

Blood eased onto my white plate too
and I thought then of what we'd said
before your gift of the liquid

bag of breasts. In your new workshop
a snowball of deer blood had melted
onto a stretch of paper. The blood

was vermilion, shockingly *there*.
We shared a recall of the Arctic,
of caribou butchered on snow.

That blood on the fresh snow,
how beautiful it was and how
the hunters' artistry gave us

our memories intact. Blood. Mud.
Every day working with what you find –
your sketch books too, drawn in mud.

Fitting then to find here a ghost
of Rembrandt's rack of beef, even
Chardin's eviscerated skate.

And, for me, to contemplate words
and the silence they're pulled from –
and how they end up on the plate.

Caravaggio in Dumfries

On the first ever day of spring, Caravaggio
strolls over the old stone bridge to market.

There, he orders three pounds of pippins,
two of red delicious, one each of bananas

and of pears. His eye tells him what's ripe,
what's sweet, crisp or tart. Lastly, he points

to a large bunch of inky-blue grapes. *Per favore.*
'Nice ones these,' remarks the vendor –

a tiny lady in a black Bulls cap with one
winking gold tooth. She's noticed how

taken her customer is with the grapes.
Caravaggio thinks he'll paint them later,

include them in his knowing *Little Bacchus* –
that sallow-skinned portrait of his self.

He is twenty or so – fresh from the country –
and what he feels this warming morning

standing before these piled fruit stalls
is not innocence but wide-eyed appetite –

an openness to all fecundity. History
will call him *stormy petrel*, tempestuous,

libidinous; temper as much as fever
will eventually kill him. But this morning

all that feels so unlikely; impossible even,
as he heads for home, cradling his five bags of fruit.

At the bridge head, one of a pair of swans,
circling its young, raises itself from the river

and lifts up its wings. A slab of white light
hits Caravaggio with a shock of pleasure

like a lover's open thigh, a magnificence
that folds in on itself, as indeed light folds

into darkness. A lesson his eye takes in
before he returns across the sparkling waters.

Simon in the Vegetable Patch

At the end of rows of runner beans –
perfect, proud, erect – your peas,
equally perfect and sweet as I remember –

a taste in tact from childhood –
lie in a tangle of their own devising.
With a bundle of canes like pick-up-sticks,

a ball of twine, a knife as red
as a rooster's comb whose blade
winks in the sun, you spend an afternoon

half-hour; no real notion
what you're doing, only what you want
to achieve – to bring those peas to order!

You think in planes, in angles,
in zigs and zags: a stage set for peas
to shine like blades, to lift themselves

onto open palms. Somehow it's disaster.
But at least it's half an hour
when not much else is happening.

Your daughter tops a white cap
with sunshine, her eyes the centre
of all that is: a picture that spirals

beyond her mother, her mother's friends,
the busy hens, the pony that stands,
head bowed in private penance;

out yet to green maps of alder and ash
that ripple with health till the blue sky
clips them. But at last, hey ho,

a solution. Your blade rides
through knotted twine; you amass
an airy pile of branches. 'Something

more . . . *informal,*' you say. Too late!
The company calls on you – a walk
to the grey, roiling sea. And sweetly

you accept, though there'll be nothing to show
for this half hour of all your labours –
as there's nothing to show

for half an hour when your daughter
sat in the sun and smiled and laughed
at her mother, her mother's friends,

the busy hens, the penitent pony,
and the ash, the alder, the rows
of runner beans and peas where her father

worked carefully, without care,
puzzling over a tiny piece of green chaos
while there was order everywhere.

Mushrooms

West Cork, Ireland

Today in the lee of the islands of Sherkin,
Castle, Calf, Clear and Hare, the small island
of Skeam East turns like a ragged butterfly
in a blue, wingless sea. Roaring Water Bay

can never have seemed so inaptly named.
In the fields above the island ruins, Dan and I,
the sun on our shirtless backs, pick mushrooms
in an idly purposeful way. They're everywhere,

extended families of milky white heads
shining in the summer's still cropped green.
And the houses, I ask – a scatter of stone husks
above the landside bay – when were they

abandoned? Hard to say: famine some; others
as late as the fifties. A hundred years or so
of a drifting death. I'm pulled to the island's
furthest edge, fooled by a handful of bone-

white crab shells. Water slaps into beaker-
smooth gulleys. An open boat chugs past, the dull
plops of lobster pots measuring the silence.
Together we fill a bucket with mushrooms

and cache them in a mesh of broken ferns;
then go off in search of more, strolling
aimfully through the open fields, leaving few
for those who'll come after. 'Stuff 'em!'

I agree. Later as our families trail back
across the spit of land to where Dan's boat
tugs at the slightly less sandy beach, I idle
in a ruin, crouching below the rafters'

stone slots. The small windows have turned
from the landscape around them. Like a vegetable
beneath a box bed, I am brushed by the spores
of a shadow life the light can't touch.

That night our cornucopia of mushrooms
boil down into a mess of slippery ashes,
into the salty, blue-black ink of themselves.
Their juices colour everything they touch

with a fisherman's dye. It's the colour
of cold hearths, of a louring sky, of the grit
at the sea's edge after the storm has passed
and the Wreckers' eyes shine in the darkness.

Island Love

You walk up from the strand, your creel brimming
with herring; you come down from the hill,
your creel laden with turf, your grey-green eyes
cast down on the stony path, your black hair

wet with sweat or a moil of salty mist;
and glad am I there's a bond between us
for it seems to me I'm a poor catch
for this world. My fishing lines tangle and break

in calm waters, lobsters climb from my pots
to go seeking greater challenge elsewhere;
when the sea heaves and gurls black, I'm the first
to lose hope. I set sail with hymns on my lips.

Others there are that would have built for you
a better house; stones that knitted tightly
against the bitter wind, capped with a roof
the hens couldn't lay in. Such men would have turf

stacked for ten winters and then turf to spare;
men to make you proud their knowledge was sought,
their courage praised: for did they not leap
Bull's Cove for you, from black rock to black rock,

as down below fulmars wheeled and the white
water thundered in? They did? God bless them!
But you have a dreamer, a grim fisher
in melancholy; an idler who stares

into the tell-tale smoor of the fire, his tale
often the heaviest creel you carry.
Feckless, your father called me, *indolent*,
your mother: our tongue is rich in name-tags.

Your love is a mystery and a blessing.
No matter where the black dogs take me,
towards overhang or scree, you guide me
back to clear tracks of sunlight; constantly

giving our lives the shape of the journey
they are on. You make plans for the market
and provision for each birth. You let faith
take care of the rest – a deep faith that shines

in those bright grey-green eyes, a faith that sees
the lines of my life when I do not,
that welcomes me dripping from the dark sea
when we give up our tired white bodies with joy.

At *La Poivière*

At *La Poivière*, the old words come to me –
the soft plosives of *bower* and *bough* –
as I stand below a fiery vault
of cherries. In the filtered sunshine,
first I hold the ladder for my son
as he reaches up to another bright cluster
and drops them in the bowl. And as he does,
so I reach out from the heart of the tree
and feed on those perfect little planets,
coldly burning, which orbit his ankles.

But you're clamouring for your chance too
to harvest plenty, to pluck a treasure
so willing it makes us needlessly laugh.
Soon, your industry's sending our son
running for 'Something! Anything!' Nothing
will stop you now, as you toss down
handfuls for me to hold for the coming bowl.
Only I don't. Part-hidden from you
by one of those leafy boughs, I slip
the cherries, one by one, into my mouth.

With tongue and teeth, I ease out the stone
and the sweet flesh is gone by the time
I spit the pit into the dry earth
or at the crumpled green handkerchiefs
of lettuce. You will, after all, pick more
than my hand or a bowl will bear.
And when you do, I'll reach out again
around your skirts to harvest whatever
falls within my reach; thinking, somewhere here
is a parable concerned with love or beauty.

Rainy Day Mayenne

Rain falls on the brindled cows
composed within their loose pen of poplars;

on the empty duck pond with its square,
flat-bottomed boat. While quadrilles of chestnuts

and limes shoulder the storm, you
blow soap bubbles into the sherry-dark.

Sizeable fruits they are, each one at least
an apple, though now and again, a sweet

little cantaloupe, almost waisted, falls
from your hooped lips. We marvel

at your steady puckered breath; at the soft
watery explosions, the meaningless

blessings we reach for with our open palms –
'let it come! *let it come!*' – as outside rain falls

on the lonely old roads, on churches spaced
like stations – see, in each, St Joan rising

cleanly from flaming tracks. And rain falls
on the war memorials, each name a prayer –

never again – and on the villages
where geraniums disburse their brilliant mould

round windows, doors and walls. I love you
unencumbered like this –

lost in what you do.
                    Outside a buzzard,
carved from a fence post, takes off

in the drizzle and looks down on a landscape
held by the seams of Roman roads

and by the ramparts of chestnuts and limes,
now shimmering in a rain-stopping light.

On Hearing of Your Illness

So how did it happen? Twenty five years
of friendship – not one minute of it
on foreign soil (and no love letter
till this). The closest we came, the past

glorious summer in the west. We lived it
without doors at Ravenstone, surrounded
by sycamore and beech so richly green
not a breath of wind touched us; the corn

ripened at our backs beneath a sun
that made each day its predicate. We drove
one afternoon to a beach on the Mull,
down hot little roads slashed by sunlight

and shadows, to find a white eiderdown
of mist had rolled over the Irish Sea.
I picnicked in the moony sun, digging
my heels into the sand, while I watched you

wade into the mist, poised as if you bore
a clay pot on your head through heat and dust;
and emerge from it too as if time hadn't
touched you in all those years, your body

a companion piece to your teenage son's.
You waved then to a world composing itself
in those brown otter-bright eyes. That summer
anyone with a boat pulled mackerel

from the glassy bay. Freezers were stacked
with them, yet each day brought fresh offers.
On my last night at Ravenstone, we cooked
the petrol shiny fish on a wood fire,

the flesh so white, so fresh it fairly crumbled
in your hands. We shared a grassy mound,
a rowdy crowd of renegades, our air
suffused with sweet smells of woodsmoke

and marijuana. It was, let's say,
Wigtownshire exotic! Some months later,
I heard of the phosphorus bombs raked
from Beaufort's Dyke: 4,000 fire-sticks,

caked with decades of rust that littered
these pilgrim shores. And I recalled a slight
unsteadiness as you'd waved from the sea's edge,
before that clouded landscape took you to its heart.

Survivors

Dumfries and Galloway, Spring 2001

We stepped out cautiously
after such a long penning, our joints
stiff, our eyes stung by sunlight. Yet the field –
how green it was! – the lush turf
tucked into each of its corners.
And oh, for us then, each blade of grass,
each swell of thistle,
each mooning buttercup,
was an untrodden joy. At first
it seemed as if our whole world
lay before us, field upon field –
each trimmed in white
by a celebrant hawthorn –
and we would move through them
on strengthening legs
till sea pinks marked the edge
of our kingdom. These were truly
blissful moments. But brief.
For, after the first sweetness of air
wore off (for such a time we'd known
nothing but the heat
of our own confinement)
our nostrils sensed something else
riding the spring air; a weave
of drifting smoke, the sour brand
of burning flesh. And then
the stories drifted our way too,
of the nervous waiting, the moaning,
the screaming; the dull thud,
the slump of death.
And of the huge pyres that lit up
the night sky; blackened limbs
thrust out like plate racks.
Nothing it seemed could save the chosen –

no pleading, no tears. There are more
crows in most fields now
than the placid, soft eyed creatures
you liked to pass. Fat and black,
they trip over their own good fortune.
They remind us, whatever happens now,
we're all living on borrowed time.

Pilgrim

When you arrive at the White Loch of Myrton,
that's not the end of your journey, though
for the time you are there it may seem so.

For the White Loch will say, Lay it down –
why don't you? – the tired old rhetoric of self.
Contradiction, sophistry, hope or regret –

shove it all overboard like a lump
of machinery that's never quite made sense;
that's simply been something for you to work on.

Even now as it slips behind the scene,
the one you've called, 'White Loch of Myrton',
you feel how its arcane circuits absorb you.

But *you* are something altogether different,
sitting on a smooth rock-stool by the water's edge,
as so-slow bees drone between buttery blobs

of ragwort and trout click their watery tongues
whenever your back is turned. You are not
the heavy load you've cast aside. You share

instead something of the deep unruffled
stillness of the water, the bluish haze
of bulrushes, the load line between the trees

and their reflections. Hold to that lightness
and see how easy it is to love at the White
Loch of Myrton, where you have no history

but this moment. Still you'd be a fool
if you thought the White Swan of Myrton
would find any of this lovable in you.

And you were a fool to think you could love her.
Tending three dowdy chicks almost as big
as herself, she spits into your reverie:

Go refreshed, she says, but remember,
pilgrim, you cannot live forever on the edge
of the White Loch of Myrton.

Landscapes

There is a time in life when you just take a walk:
And you walk into your own landscape.
(from Sketchbook 1: Willem de Kooning, 1904–1997)

1

Dense rhododendron bushes almost mask
the start of the track. Oak boughs cast

shadows on sunlit days across it. Ferns
grow unchecked. Once milk churns

and linen passed by to the Big House
and, halfway along, a walled garden still shows

raspberries like spinning tops. The iron door
lies open. Within these walls, desire

rises in you like sap. The world pounds
with green fire: *find me*, you pray, *find me*.

2

Ferns break apart on your shins and thighs;
sand runs so quickly through your toes,

it tells of no time but this instant,
on a helter-skelter, cool, green-tented

path to the sea. As if it were red hot rock,
you take the crumbly seaweed; lock, stock

and barrel, leap driftwood and the clear mines
of jellyfish (for once with no questions) –

till the cold brine takes you and expels you
and teaches you all the body's truths anew.

#3

The air is smoky with an early haar
as your father, hen basket in hand,

strides up the hill to a suburban
country track, where he stoops over such rare

dandelion heads, at their milky fullest,
their leaves fall from them in long green straps.

For your white rabbits, the best of the crop.
And how fresh is his gift! Lightly pressed

in the basket, greenness unfurls:
on taut skin, you stencil a string of pearls.

#4

One after another, they fall from his hand
onto the ground; and, as we look, the only sound

is of paper brushing paper like a beat,
each beat equal to the eye. They are Light,

Colour and Movement – seaweedy, swampy; or fields
in the early morning, tinder dry, but folded

under haze. At first they are unnamed, his hand
drawing them from the landscapes of his mind.

The best are like staring into a busy pond.
You can stay with one longer by raising your hand.

#5

The lilac drops, so full in the dusk,
you let it brush your lips, let it mask

the face you give only to evening;
to laurel, dark as an old engraving

of rain. Out of its thick hatching, the bright
orange light of a blackbird's beak

draws you on. To follow its rhythms
is to fill your mouth with a song of earth:

as night falls, to see the distant hills dusted
with a purple that's closer to rust.

#6

On the sea-floor, at midnight, brown, bulbous weeds
wave their gloved fingers; sharp-edged reeds

reach for the softness of sky. Spotted
yellow birds, bright as candles, are dotted

around me, their fish-eyes black as night.
Out of the forest's underwater moonlight,

once more below a deep, dark, sea-blue sky,
I come to a town that cannot fool me.

Its towers are numinous fish bones;
its beaked flags are prized open in song.

#6 draws on two landscapes by Paul Klee: *Landscape with Yellow Birds*
and *Flagged Town*.

#7

In *his* Welsh landscape, all was organ sound;
a perpetual spring clotted the gravid land.

No wonder he'd difficulty with Death –
and Time. Not so the priest who burnished

each line – a ship; sleek, swift, sure – sent out
to the furthest shore. Or the dean who minted

rhymes from the body's song, the soul's voyage.
I've never understood you, W.S.G.,

but, in the dark watches of the night, there's
your small, clear voice talking to your father.

#8

Who was your father died a long time ago –
and now lies through the programmed doors

lit like a hologram – a landscape
of the mind; though his eyelids are mapped

with blue ink and shaving nicks still glower
with crumbs of blood. You want to ease down the nap

of his dry lips, but when you stoop, fear
you'll pass right through his body's thick flow

of light. Instead, you stub your lips on a head
smooth and cold as a tide-washed stone.

#9

Each of us is born on an open field,
yet we die in a forest.
Polish proverb.

One with a nondescript but muddy track,
somewhere on the border of an eastern bloc,

whose ill-paid guards have long absconded.
One in whose deep, boggy reaches, wounded

but shapely as tongues, boats have surfaced.
The low croon of ancient voices is laced

through the trees. One, as children, we wandered
into. In the fir-mirk, you tag your father,

his cap on backwards, whooping between trees,
running ever further into darkness.

#10

In the middle of the park, an obelisk
of rough-hewn granite grows out of the mist.

There's nothing elegant about it. What-
ever it commemorates, you forget.

It's ringed, equally, by love and by hatred.
The indifferent hand of childhood now lifts

the chained metal cup to the waterspout
sunk in its heart. There's a muffled shout.

Too late! Your lips take the first icy sip —
and then you are old, remembering it.

#11

When the giant hillside beech was torn down
by its own weight, or weight of the storm it found

more malleable than it, it lay raw and wounded,
its stars of roots and the earth laid bare. A loom

of well-worn tracks became useless; the mulch
of the forest was bruised, dug into, till the pulse

of the shock, it seemed, slowed and once more growth,
nimble rooted, asserted itself. Tall foxgloves

flourish now in the shade of the trunk, and ferns
lock onto sunlight with hungry green thorns.

#12

These thick old webs are patternless, anarchic.
One holds a louse like a water beetle

swimming to no-surface. A moth sticks
to the glass like a seed head leaked

from the outside; a world that's level with it —
of light shredded by nettles with dark

leathery leaves and purple stems. Pebble chip
spiders on threadlike legs work

secretly here. The crimson woundwort suggests
each flower is an extravagance, a hooded dress.

#13

Driftwood. What does it take that you should love it?
That it be warped, stripped, or like this: burnt

beyond use, its topography weathered
smooth. Or various like this; this rusted

charred piece of a lobster pot – nails and twine
fused in a handspan the sea saved: in time

that you should love it, for being useless.
You can't make more of me than I am, it says.

Good for burning. Hold me,
like someone with no more salt tears to cry.

#14

The lights are all out. The wind passes
whispering by you, leaving traces

of voices you will not hear again.
It's summer by the light of your moon:

sand dunes cast shadows like perfect fans.
So what did you lose on that beach? Whose hand,

cold as the North Sea, wakes you tonight?
Let it go, let it go. Let me be a noust

for you. A curse on that landscape's bitter cry.
The lights are all out. The wind passes me by.

#15

The empty bell. The dead birds in the house
beat in your breast. Whatever's upset them,

the coming storm, a call they cannot answer,
the peace you thought you'd bought for them – a truce

that's now been broken – you feel their wings rise
against your heartbeat, their small bones swerve

and swerve again, feathering their dying panic.
Deep, in the small black rocks

of their eyes, are windows onto fields and sky –
and the darker rocks against which their wings tire and break.

#16

No spring this evening. No fruits under the leaves.
James Wright's line, *I have wasted my life,*

plays through your mind. The river is flooded,
but one bridge seems as good as another

to watch the thick braids of muddy water,
the broken trunk, the tyre, the youngbloods

drive down to see. You shuffle through other nights,
other landscapes, but can't re-make the map

that led to this cold balustrade
along lineaments of fiction and of hope.

#17

The lamp is a heart, emptying itself
across your desk. If you've any wealth

you'll find traces of it here: the bright cheeks
of worthless objects, fruits from withered stalks.

Your friend, the adventurer's sailed away.
(Pieces of driftwood, tokens, history.)

In all things weighty, he worries he's light.
But you'll write him a letter. You'll post it tonight.

Over the clear white paper on your desk,
the heart is a lamp, emptying itself.

#18

Fionnghal sails home from Carolina.
Contact with death's turned her from minor

actress into something much darker.
Tears like Finnan haddies hang from her;

each marks a son lost in a wildwood war,
far from this hold with its foul beds of heather.

She knows now that dandy's accent made no sense –
a landscape at odds with its audience –

and wonders how her own travels will sound
once her vowels open up back on home ground.

Note: Fionnghal is Gaelic for Flora

#19

When you drink water, think about the source,
the Chinese say. One reason to travel.

So, with the proper dispensations,
and a new breed of horse – hot-blooded, large-

lunged – we fought through thunder, lightning and hail
to reach the Heartland. Each night wolves

attacked our camp. Eagles tracked us. All the way
to a marshy field, a non-place; a barren core.

Enlightened, I took note: *The source is where*
                                    the river's not there anymore.

#20

You tell me there's a path if I simply look.
But the clearest route to it's blocked

with black, boggy mud; pools so dark
and inert, insects score them like pencil marks.

How do I trust those spongy stacks of turf?
If one gives, will I have enough

spring in my step to make the next uncertainty?
And the path itself advances with such shy

hopes up the mountain – a mere trickle of sand –
only to find clouds drowned in a blue tarn.

#21

Not much of a climb to overlook the town –
a track, a field, its stanky edges pounded

down by spring rains. Soon we turn from slopes
smooth as colanders, and the town's dropped,

polished and glowing, five miles away.
A lochan nestles close by, and a colony

of gulls take turns to rise and to settle
like the molecules on a potter's wheel.

Rising *within us* on that green hilltop –
words yet to be spoken; the seedhead, hope.

#22

Nothing they found clad darkness better than stone.
In such darkness only they felt safe and warm,

for then it was theirs to control. Our days
are spent touring such spots: the gentle rise

of homes and tombs, like beehives opened
up to light. On the beach, we too blend

smooth stones in a ritual of play which
somewhere goes beyond that into a rich

imagining. At night I rise above a nest
covered with rooty turf. I enter the darkness.

#23

The willow herb's a purple wash
out the corner of my eye. Tall firs rush

up hillsides and are gone. Steadily,
we climb to the river's source as the valley

darkens with heather. The children collapse
into sleep; your head tips back. I fill the gap

between you and the world. The flat-faced owl
clocks me, swivels his head, and hauls

himself up into the stunned air. I wake
at night and wonder whose foot is on the brake.

#24

We took him to a house on the coast
(he dreamed) and then were lost

to him for twenty days. He didn't like it
one bit. At night the house slipped

under the sheet of the sea and he slept.
And he dreamed of a clapboard house, tipped

towards the on-coming tide, and of a boy
who sat alone there at a squint window

for whom the sea-light, dying, looked –
and felt – like the closing of a book.

#25

In the undimmed light of summer, bats
circle round your back door – the tail ends

of stories that can't get home.
                          Bats, or more truly,
memories of bats: wings like dead dockens,

furry faces beyond love. In his sleep,
your son speaks of a house. You pause

at its door like a thief. It shimmers, then sinks
without trace. It had jewels. It had claws.

Bats. They circle round your back door –
the tail ends of stories you can't reach anymore.

#26

You pass through to the world of shades, there to meet
with your former lovers. They stand aside

from their present households, their skin glowing,
their bodies those of the youths you knew.

You cannot speak of the longings that brought you here.
You cannot speak of who your presence might betray.

Your former lovers – palms up – feel for rain;
then return to their homes, to their children.

Mothers with grey flecked hair, who've forgotten
whatever it was you once loved in them.

#27

I pack her bags with the most precious things –
love, desire; fear woven through it all like song.

But I don't trust her. I hold up a mirror
to her face. I tell her she's a picture.

But I don't believe in her. She leaves me.
I like to think it's mutual. Now we're both free.

But I find myself thinking of her at night.
My words hover at the edge of prayer.

She knocks on my window, wide-eyed, unslept –
a sprig of vomit in her tangled up hair.

#28

I've walked through slaughterhouses,
where birds sing, butterflies jerk through the air.

I've stood beneath shining birch trees,
where bodies tumbled, blood poured over matted hair.

When I move through innocent fields,
horror follows – torture and hidden graves.

I live on blood's doorstep and study
all the ghastliness from which I've been saved.

For this, all the lives I've yet to grieve for
haunt me, as I pass, bearing peace or war.

#29

Lost, he sees the city as a fluid
maze of grey stone, cradled by the ruins

of avenues, the geometry of parks
that chaptered his youth. In dreams, he marks

the special places — an alleyway or clock —
beyond which the city lies, a grim and broken-

backed book. In autumn he returns.
The city shines in sunlight. It's turned

from all the old warnings. Yet what fire,
what eroticism, distance lends desire!

#30

The clouds are high and hard and you are high
above them, looking for that patch of blue

to pass through, through which you'll catch the patchwork
of fields; then a river freckled

with fallen leaves. The ache of fear's so like
the ache of loneliness you had for years —

such a cack-handed gift to yourself! Gripped
by clouds that could rip

your frail craft apart, you sense, as you pass,
a heart flowing free of bitterness at last.

Section Three

Legacies

Hector

One morning, the curtains open,
sunlight and spices on sea air

are scattered over his parents'
dishevelled bed. Only his mother

lies there now, a half empty cup
of wine by her side. Nightmare's

brought him to their bed again –
trees on fire; animals running

in panic from the liquid flames.
His father moves around elsewhere

whistling like a forest, poring
over old campaigns; when, part hug

part game, he begins to roll a finger
round one of his mother's nipples.

The warm nightdress slides from it,
this way and that, as the nipple

thickens. The nightdress is a pale
straw yellow but perhaps that's

confusing it with an earlier memory –
the creamy goodness it once cloaked.

They both explore the moment now;
she watching him with a half smile,

sharing these small gifts of pleasure
with her dearest son.
     It will be years

before he'll know that breast again.
Standing on the doomed walls of Troy,

his mother, begging him through tears
to evade Achilles' wild grief,

loosens her dress and holds the breast
out to him on her palm – the breast

in the glare of that moment, the most
tender, the most eloquent feature

in the whole dry landscape of war.
Hector recalls, as she begs him to,

how as a child he'd been suckled
and soothed by the same shriven breast –

and the death-marked hero's almost
disarmed by the sweetness of that

distant memory: till it comes
back to him – the glimpse he'd once had

of something other, equally
nourishing, a time when he'd turned

and walked with her back in-
to a burning forest, to find the fire

moulded itself around them and birds
were singing through the flames.

The Football

One spring, Dad came home from school
with an old football the gymies
wanted shot of. A real football, mind –

not one of your plastic ones,
but with a teat that sprang up
from the pink bladder, and trembled

between hexagons of rough leather.
Aye, it's a good one that: which is what
he liked to say of anything

that could bear it. Oh and this ball
had seen service! Did they not
kick ones just like it at the Somme?

I stubbed my toes, launching it
into flower beds where it flattened
all it touched. Then when

lammed into the apple trees,
it rained blossom. Banished at last,
I took it to the park with friends

aware of my limitations.
But then other boys came, laughing
up the slope – confident, at ease.

Any game? His ball. *Can we play?*
I sulked on the line as they kicked
the leather off my ball. Later

I carried it home, a stranger's
bloody head, and threw it, clattering,
deep into the shadows of the hut.

Curds

It was a Sunday thing – four bowls
of rennet and milk on the cupboard top
behind the kitchen door. There was mystery
to it, a base alchemy that could
turn this liquid into something so solid
the hull of a spoon could sail across it.

It wasn't like the warm milk I pumped
to butter in a croft house or the way
milk whipped to cream when suddenly the moment
came and the elements turned. There was more
to it than that. In science once, we grew
a copper sulphate crystal. Mine, the size

of a baby's fist, was daggerlike,
startlingly blue. I toted it round the teachers
as told, but felt the talisman I bore –
time given shape and colour in a jar –
was closer to religion than to science.
So with curds, to let time work, Mum told us

'Keep the door shut! They'll never set
in a draft.' I saw ripples breaking over
their distracted surfaces, spiking that
concentration I've seen since on faces
desperate to come. And then the moment
was lost – and the plates of milk, waste.

But when it worked, four full moons were set
before us with a jug of cream and a pot
of nutmeg. As our spoons hefted a clean
wedge of curd, the speckled cream oozed
into its space. Oh sister, what's soothed since
like the placid geisha faces of our youth?

The Card Players

After the luxury of advocaat, lapped
from one-shot glasses held like nuggets
in our fists, we cluster round the orange light
of the paraffin lamp as the cards are dealt.

For a few nights after my aunt and uncle
have left, we'll play on: Sweaty Betty mostly.
Mum loves to say the name. It's terrible!
Like those other words that have escaped

from *Down Below* where language is fiery
or viscous. We are not, I don't think,
a Games Family but play the hands out
as our heavy reading chairs hunker

in the darkness and the lamp's flame
creeps up till a black feather of smoke
presses itself against the glass funnel.
Between hands I make the shortest walk

to the blind gable end of the cottage.
From here ferns thicken to a real darkness
though the track is still held by light swells
of broom. I piss on the grass; my soft

ssh blurring with the steady burr
of the burn. The stars thicken also –
teased out wool caught on the barbs
of their constellations. For a moment

I'm giddy. When I walk back round
I glimpse the card players past the thin
print curtains; their backs are almost black,
their open faces cut like diamonds

in the lamplight. My cards lie face down
on the table, waiting for me to play them.
Beside them, my father stands, tightening
the top of a hot water bottle.

Woman Hanging out the Washing

by Camille Pissarro

Bonnard's wife never aged in his eyes.
Again and again he paints her down the years,
as a filament that lights up her tub,
or svelte as a teenager as she towels
the tall vase of a calf. In recompense

she treated him like shit, his tribute
rather a trap. On the other hand,
Pissarro here takes a break from painting
orchards with flowering fruit trees, peasants
glowing with an earthy vigour, to catch

Madame Pissarro (it's only a guess)
with a child and barrow load of washing.
She is teasing out a sheet on the line
while turning her head to look past her arm
down at the golden haired toddler, patient

as a book-end, on the warm summer grass.
How *our* mother hated, or said she did,
our father's domestic scenes. To be caught
peeling apples, ironing – uncomposed,
exposed, she felt, in the darg of her day.

What could be less true? 'I am melancholy,
harsh and savage in my works,' Pissarro
exclaims to Lucien, his eldest child
of six; and he pins this woman's profile –
art within art – on the canvas of the sheet.

There's a photograph I took from the kitchen
of our small walled garden on a summer's day;
like Pissarro's, the hedge a full rich green,
nasturtium leaves like lilies and the whole
suffused with a dancing, shadowy light.

It was months before ruined arteries
cost Mum both her legs. Our son crawls across
the patchy grass as *Grandmère* lifts a white sheet
from a blue plastic basket, hands it over
so that you may peg it on the line.

How slow her legs were then! – her feet inching
over the dry earth, yet what reflected joy
was in her insistence to be useful.
Next year she will try gently to explain
to my father they have no Home but this

one room in an old brick house at the end
of a sycamore lane. Young Titi,
if Titi it is, basking in the gaze
of his mother, will die, aged twenty-three
in London, of TB: *our poor Titi*

that we loved so much . . . He was an artist.
And you Camille, living from hand to mouth,
dressing wounds in sunlight, did your long life
ever look so solid, or a child so safe?
How you must have thought of this moment

and wished you could simply lay down your brush,
scratch your enormous beard and step outside,
not into a world lost to time or to art,
but into the clear light of Pontoise to hoist
that child, one more time, high over your head.

Island Room

In a rambling house on a distant island,
I've heard there's a room, one half of it curtained
from the other by chicken wire. In this half
there's an upturned lobster boat called *Lucky*. Pigeons

use it as a perch; chickens like to roost there. Light
from the windows catches feathers when flight stirs them
or filters through the rusting wire to shine
on the droppings mottling the shell of a boat

the way of lichen on a fallen menhir.
The threadbare chairs are evenly divided, so
you can sit in silence, should you choose, and watch
the world you are coming to and will always reach

in time. Of course it's possible to ignore all this
domestic eccentricity, to put your hand
clean through the wire, to grasp another's, your father's
say, invariably chilled, his nails rough as bark

but the hand itself still the hand of your father,
broad and bearing the ghost of capability,
though you find it lying on his lap like a bird's
limited foot. And you can sit and look where he looks,

and where your mother looks too, at the unfocused
horizon and try to remember all the names
of the wildflowers she taught you: *This is the Star
of Bethlehem, this Thrift, and this Solomon's Seal.*

Now are you listening? And are you listening yet? –
as vase upon vase tips over your outstretched hands,
slips through your fingers – the faded heads
                              and yellowed stems.
From such as these you'll pleat for yourself a mother.

Mostly though you sit in silence as feathers fall
through sunlight till the walls of the room and the room
itself seem the most fragile of ideas. 'Quick now,'
you may have heard your father say at such a time,

'another before your mother comes.' And then both
you and he sink into your chairs, to feel the warmth
of each other's presence – your breathing, his sipping –
your idle thoughts drifting through the grid of days

till his smile latches onto something so fleeting
it's like a feather's caught over his mouth and been
brushed from it in an instant. I think if you were
simply to take a deep breath and walk through the wire

you'd find yourself – as I do – in such a brittle world,
twigs snapping under your feet, gathering themselves
into scattered piles of dusty breaks and fractures,
the stour would catch at the back of your throat or brush

your cheeks like the first warm flurries of snow that come
from nowhere. But soon enough you'd settle to silence,
to those wings folded to perfection, to pink lids closing
on a room I can find no words to leave quietly.

My Father's Funeral

It's the first frosty day in November,
a day pure as a walk along Dornoch beach,
when all the brush strokes are clear – each wave
of sand, of sea, each twirl of wispy cloud –
and your nose to the canvas all the way
to Embo. 'Bonnie.' Aye, bonnie right enough.
Today though, it's the Pennines I cross
to reach you: they lapping, silver on green,
below a sky *you'd* call 'cerulean blue' –

it's almost a shock, Dad, the day's
painted with such a full palette.
Then, arriving at the first staging post
to the grave, in the close family hubbub,
it's no surprise to find you not there,
preferring instead a private moment's
vanity in the long hall mirror, rubbing
your moustache with delight at how black
suits you – you and those flashing brown eyes!

Later, as we wait beside the sleek hearse
for *Agnes*, you go walkabout again –
an absence you can conjure anywhere
(the tuneless whistle, the stamping dance) –
caught between contemplation of your shoes
and the waiting of a man at the end
of a million accumulated waitings,
a man who can't possibly wait longer –
till, 'Ah, here she comes now. *Michty me*! –

what kept her?' addressing a top-hatted
pall-bearer, his northern accent so rich,
the gravity of the occasion flies from us
and we share a conspiratorial wink.
It's after, I catch you glancing across
at the grave-diggers, leaning on their shovels
under bare oak trees, sharing a joke,

their job half done. And that's where I think
you'd like to be now, anticipating

the punchline, or simply watching them
handle a spade. Country boy at heart,
how you loved to watch anybody
do something well. But, suddenly it's over:
the singing, the prayers, and the tears.
                                        You're last
to leave the graveside, turning away,
just when the copper sun angles itself
to perfection; picks out your brass nameplate
and our first scatterings of dry earth.

Poppies

This is how I want to paint,
my mother said and pointed
to her poppies i.e. not

with any kind of Victorian exactitude –
a timidity that never
dared to interpret

what stood in the vase before her.
Her poppies loom blowsily
out of the frame; strain

on their stems, their pistils golden
with fertility or lust.
                        There's nothing
Plathian about them either:

these are no rags, no wounds
shaming the air. They leave
the dead world behind them.

Note how space parts for them
with joy. They are joy. Too heavy
to sway, they nod gently –

Where? Not on Flanders Field
but in a southern breeze –
exotic, bold; precious

as the armfuls of wild white lilies
I bore once round Cape Town
like a swaddled child.

And as if no heavier
than those lilies, I gathered up
my dead mother,

her face already waxen,
in my arms. Her soul –
lighter still –

rose steadily in the currents
of an unseasonal winter warmth,
fierce as a flame;

free as one of the painted poppies
it had wanted to be
all along.

For the Poets

1. THE BIRD MAN

For Alastair Reid

He is a man fluent
in the language of origami —
an eloquent *esperanto*
of the hands. Present him
with any size or shape
of paper — however flimsy,
however ragged — he'll trim it,
fold it, fashion for you
a bird; in any language,
it's a bird. Personally,
I've observed him
at work in the dark
of a rolling taxi, in the damp-
handed tropics and at a cramped
dinner table with heads nodding
over his articulate hands.
Grip the chest, he'll tell you,
once it's finished, *and gently*
tug the tail. In and out.
In and out. The wings flap;
jerkily, it's true, but still
the bird, in any language,
comes alive. More so
when he says, *All it needs now*
is an eye. Here. And here.
A black dot stares
across the crowded table
from that moment on.
Though all in all,
the making's the thing:
for this bird — this elementary,
unambiguous bird —
lives in *his* hands, chafes
at his fingertips, to be made

flesh, to change meaning,
as it must when it takes
flight for love, or simply
to fill all the moments
when there's nothing better
to do than magic. And this bird,
which has sung for its supper
in so many languages,
in so many circumstances,
is perhaps the smallest
of his many accomplishments,
yet it is, nevertheless, a constant
that flies between languages
with all its possible messages –
and that goes easily and eloquently
where words lie pinioned.

2. ELEGY FOR THE FROG POET

i.m. Norman MacCaig

When you said that was it –
your last word on frogs
and positively too –

that was it for us all. So
when I met a frog one night,
idling at the lights, metallic,

sharp-edged on a wet pavement,
my thoughts turned only
to salvation. Besides

I'd little idea just what
a slippery subject a frog
could turn out to be.

Perhaps it would've sat there,
four-square, for the Frog Poet,
but when I bent to finger

the Braille of its back with second-
hand affections, it shot off
into the squatting queue of cars.

Held now by their lights,
and Buster Keaton white,
I bobbed between them

after my revved up quarry
like someone caught on a TV
shoot-out. At the very last

I risked offence and grasped
the sand-filled sock of a frog —
no sooner into the action

than spiralling out of it,
as the traffic began to flow;
the frog no sooner mine

than it was leaping the wall
onto the front lawn of a Home
for the Elderly, leaving me,

a split second, frozen
in drizzle, offering an invisible
bouquet to the silent stars.

3. THE HAW BUSH

i.m. Iain Crichton Smith

At a loch's edge, after heavy rain,
I stood before a haw bush, loosely woven
to let in all the light there was
of a landscape of dark water, dark hills
and darkening autumn sky. Each of its embers

held to the weight of water that hung from it
harbouring the light: each drop
so perfectly poised against the darkness,
the clustered fruits formed a whole
that more than slaked a walker's thirst.

4. THE BIRTHDAY PARTY

i.m. Hamish Henderson

After the readings, in the empty hall,
their tweed elbows flowered, their hair took new life.
One sniffed the malty air, fixed, down his fine nose,
the fiddler's eyes with his. 'Play for me, boy.
Play for me.' It was the century's close

and anyone could see they were on the edge
of the Big Time – my jocose sad captains.
With a hedge school to buttress his ancient knees,
one still croaked towards the darkness, with vowels
fervent but drowning, *Freedom Come All Ye!*

After

The Wannsee Conference, Jan 20, 1942

After, in that airy room, its views
of the garden elegantly
leading down to the lake,

you can almost feel
the ghostly exhalation of breath
at the meeting's end; the way

a body, having forcefully
made its point, eases back
into its most natural

configuration. There is too
the after-echo of chairs
drawn on a polished floor.

Meetings. Meetings. Meetings.
Always the urge when they're over
to fling open doors, windows;

cold as it was then, the desire
for movement. So we walk
where they walked, feet stamping

on the gravel. We look out on
much the same scene, breathe
much the same air. And with

the main business done,
perhaps we too could have
slotted into talk of wives,

of children, holidays and dogs.
In the Room of Departures
(we trail the taxonomy

of evil), a black scarecrow
hangs from barbed wire,
accordions escort inmates

to the gallows. And a blue tit —
why should a blue tit have life
and they no breath at all? —

hammers against the light.
Its tiny, insistent heartbeat
fills my hand as I lift up

the window and throw it free —
with no reason to doubt
the frightening thing: that one of *them*

wouldn't have done likewise.
Yet soon in another room,
the stiffness gone, he

begins his paperwork
with derivative efficiency,
ensuring the latest directive

will within days be followed
all across the crumbling Reich.
And reach too far beyond it:

with a lesson that meanings
can be both given and stolen
from even the smallest things —

from blue tits, signatures, tears.

Three Masks

1

A fold, a cut, a bend, a crease
and my daughter's brought to her knees,
mooing as she nibbles the damp grass.

2

I have a nose the length of my face.
I could use it to flense a whale. Or else
to keep my mistress in the shadows.

3

Nothing of him to bury or to burn —
the skin of a pillow slip, the small warm
feathers that brush my face in a storm.

from **Legacies**

The dead are very demanding. Adam Phillips.

Every night, for my litany of the dead,
I pluck, with a sleight of hand, the sadness
that hides in kitchen talk. Next day, I'll bless
the dead friends of friends I've never seen –
what can be named won't then overwhelm me.

But Lord, there's no end to the dead!
They make a palimpsest of my list;
each name's closer than the last. They send me
running on errands for items they miss –
to the corner shop for fresh obits and bread.

The women of Terezin, brutalised
and fed on slops, transcribed recipes
for Breast of Goose, Plum Strudel, Chocolate Torte
in a *Kochbuch*. Any scraps of paper
they could find were filled with tiny writing

and carefully bound in. Perhaps memory
too marches on its stomach. The simple steps
to a bowl of leek and potato soup –
green coins tumbling from my mother's hands –
is an act of grace to mark my good fortune.

In the smoked chill of an autumn morning,
early, my father stands on the back steps,
sharpening my pencils. He holds the black horn–
handled knife lightly and the shaved wood drops
with a glitter of graphite round his shoes.

(His measured strokes made writing my pleasure.)
The penknife snaps shut. My father blows
on each point. His pride. In old age, he'll tut
over faulty wiring and the same knife
will buckle and close to cost him his life.

Mum allowed us to go with the others
guising, but not to take any gifts.
We stood and did our piece and having done,
with one hand turned down what the other offered:
our gifts – a waxy garden apple, some plums.

I stand before her grave with a basket
of fruit. The morning light sifts
through the darkness. She has heard my songs
in silence. I wait – O good as ever! –
for a secret sixpence pressed into my palm.

'Come now,' my grandpa said, 'none of your nonsense.
Out with it!' My school reading of *A Man's
A Man* my mother thought was so intense.
Grandpa sipped tea from a saucer as he listened.
I sensed my mother's discomfort for us both.

Near death he sent home his gold watch for me.
On one side of a baroque gold fob, a frisky cock
mounts a hen etched onto an oval stone block
the colour of semen. It took years to pluck them free —
those white heads squawking in the undergrowth.

My father's antique rod, unsleeved and cast
over the rivers of the Lothians,
whispered in my ear as I slept. We Pows were
fishermen, it said. Cockenzie, Port Seton,
the herring that coursed though our blood's been lost.

At Cramond, as a boy with hook and line,
I landed an eel. Like a tongue, it writhed,
dying in the dirt, as my line around it
tightened; and all but it ran towards the future
blindly, stitching the river with silver.

We left the fishing then and headed north.
Our lungs filled with coal dust. A black seam
glints in my veins from another birth
when a body much like this, though shorter lived,
was sinewy, hard, course and useful.

'Let that be a lesson!' My father turned,
head ringing, as his smiling uncle stood,
pit hammer in hand – the metal joists singing.
'Never go down the mines.' Once burned, Dad learned,
from black rock, to curse not coal dust but chalk!

On Saturday jobs, putting light bulbs in
for the toffs, *his* dad showed him how power
shaped the Eildon hills, named the dripping woods.
In the thin mist of the Yarrow, the Ettrick
and the Tweed, history was midwife.

Now, scouring a map for ancient names,
testing a circuit to animate the dead,
he hears his own name warm on his father's tongue,
and sees crows rise from an old gable end
as the van's cold engine sputters to life.

August heat. Lost up flaming avenues
of fuchsia — an old railway cottage
where nothing worked. In the fridge the butter
puddled, the tap juddered out dust. At night
I lay, sheetless, too tired to turn the pages

of my book. I thought instead, of jars
layered with dried out caterpillars; of the way
the crabs glowed when we pinned them to the grass,
baking their sweet pink flesh on the sun's spit.
Mother cried for the fortnight. I loved it.

I too remember holidays like that:
the adult talk of what didn't concern us —
damp, dirt, discomfort. And recall how the sun,
catching my jar on the jiggling train home,
fingered me for a killer. But not that one.

That's your memory, though I live there too,
poking crabs on the scorched grass; their salty deaths
somehow shared. Have words ever caught what's true
of you? Nor me. So we'd better advance
by stealth and scuttle crabwise through these lines.

Ceci n'est pas une pipe. Only part of one –
the bowl in my palm like a plum, the top
lopped off for economy. Does this sum
up prudence on my father's part? – or life
tailored to a place where ambition stops.

Years later, I watch him fiddle and suck
his dry pipe stem grey as he sits and stares
into the questions he has framed. In brief:
my dream pipe would be huge as a carnyx;
I'd create havoc with its full-bowled blare!

Dried out now, yet still old beyond his years,
Dave recalls the time he first disappeared
into a drawing. In sunlight, he'd surfaced
to find my dad's brown eyes holding him, bright
at a fledgling artist's moment of grace.

What Dave pissed away, Dad may have lost
more steadily, but the slight smile remained
for talent – no matter how hard to sustain.
And the truth is it gave more than it cost;
at times I'm wreathed by his smile as I write.

Rain trails across a river's curve . . .
In a cupboard, a dead tortoiseshell . . .
On the shelf, Han Shan . . . I wake in a cold room
laid out with a lover's clothes. Each piece calls
out to me with a memory I must tend.

Years before we meet I keep in place
such emptiness that, though I hold the strands
of the tenses and think on you hard,
still I can wake ghostlike in a cold room, rain
on a river . . . the cries of geese, passing . . .

Come again, shy as a cat, to escape
the black rack of my self, I find one limb
pinned by shame, one by regret, one blighted
by love gone sour, one so feart of the future
waves of *chi* can't get past. Yet tonight

one of my gates − Han, Shan or Po, a door
to my ethereal soul − opens. My head
lifts from my shoulders, rolls like a stone;
light pours up my back and there I am −
a fountain of wings beating in the gloom.

There we are on the wet barnacled rock
in thick, belted gaberdines, jeans rolled up
at the ankles three times. And we're laughing,
cheeks pouched like apples, with that adult
irritant laughter we just don't want to stop.

Last night I picked three heads of honeysuckle.
Each petal rolled its lip from the pistol
three times over and more; each pink finger's
sole aim to turn itself inside out. So once
we spent laughter like pollen on a dull sea air.

Dad's old song to all Mum's work: *You know me,*
I'm easy. The brows locked. The words fresh
in his silence. Challenged, he hurt: *O aye,*
he's a terrible man your father.
To the end, she tried to keep him right.

When he rocked up, to tell her he loved her,
she was terrified he'd topple her chair.
Och Tom! Liking it, though finding it
a touch risible, who'd found it
difficult being cuddled for so long.

Once, shaking him awake, my hand on the rope
of his leg, his grey head slowly surfaced
and he exhaled my name with a sweetness
only those who are truly loved can hope
to hear. Then the smile was gone from his face.

My mother told me he'd call out my name
in distress. Again I knew I was blessed
with love; until the time he set me free –
a stranger. I walked out that sunny room then
and his fierce but fleeting joy passed on to my son.

As once you held my life, knowing it all,
so now I hold yours: the gawky girlhood,
bronchitis, wartime cycling with Irene;
the Jenners' meeting with our silent dad,
with his broad artist's hands, his dark-eyed gleam.

And last, the papery breaths, the tilted
head. The day I was born was a beautiful
May day. The hospital window was filled
with blossoms. You kept that memory fresh
for me. Now I fold another into it.

All day heat has gathered in the eaves.
I open the attic window to let in
summer's first pressings; and find what breathes
between fresh vats of cut grass and warmed earth's
my Valentine lavender from your bath.

My mother's favourite. Chance keeps a dusty
posy hanging in our kitchen. Rubbed gently,
it still smells faintly of the amnion
you float in, that will live briefly on your lips
as it did on my mother's bunched fingertips.

The first summer weeks without the shadow
of their dying. Postcards lie in a packet
on the polished table: one heartbeat
and urgency passes them by. At the foot
of the garden our children play: the Cock Crow,

the Panther padding through his sunlit lair.
Later, as the huge cones of yew darken,
I slip a rotten blue nail from my toe
like a shuffled coin; marvel at the wafer
of light that the air already hardens.

Coda: Leaving the House

Whenever we left the house
for any time, Mum liked to leave
a little washing on the line –

a tea towel say or a dish clout,
just to make people think we were
merely out. Curtains she left

half closed, with blinds half down:
let the unsuspecting who called
around find us half open, half shut –

screening the brightest streaks of light
or keeping a grey day at bay.
But of course anyone who peeked

would know no one could possibly
be living there – each surface
so carefully scoured, the smallest

cloth folded by the sink. Leave it
as you'd wish to return to it
was Mum's motto. But Dad scolded

her in her absence as he packed
and re-packed the car. 'How your mother
thinks all this'll fit . . .' Dad lacked

the patient arts. And it's an in-
complete art, the art of leaving
a house. I hear my own wife start –

'What's keeping you?' while I roam round
our house, twitching at the curtains,
leaving something always undone

NOTES

HOBOES

'Hoboes' owes a debt to the system of hobo signs described in Carl G. Liungman's *Dictionary of Symbols*. 'Hobo signs . . . is a comprehensive name for a group of similar ideographic systems used for drawing or carving into trees, walls, doors, or other surfaces. Each ideogram gives specific information concerning the place where it is found. The type of signs and their meanings are influenced by the situations the vagabonds, tramps, homeless, and destitute found themselves in up to the time of the Second World War.' However, the poems are not necessarily bound to this time-scale. The first one, for example, alludes to the European dance frenzy of 1374, which began in Germany.

ISLAND LOVE

I wrote 'Island Love' after a visit to The Blasket Islands and after reading *The Islandman* by Thomas O'Crohan. But there is no Bull's Cove on the Blaskets.

PILGRIM

The White Loch of Myrton is on the pilgrim route to Whithorn. It is said Robert the Bruce visited it, in the belief its waters cured leprosy.

LANDSCAPES

In no. 7 the poets are Dylan Thomas, Gerard Manley Hopkins, John Donne and W.S. Graham.

The first lines of nos. 14, 15, 16 and 17 come from the following poems by Paul Reverdy: *Son de Cloche, Secret, Et Maintenant* and *Tard dans la Nuit*.

'I have wasted my life' (no. 16) is the last line of the American poet, James Wright's *Lying in a Hammock at William Duffy's Farm in Pine Island, Minnesota*.

No. 19 draws on a report (*Independent on Sunday*, 30 April 1995) concerning a successful expedition to find the source of the Mekong River in China.

HECTOR

The central incident in this poem is described in Book 22 of *The Iliad*, 'The Death of Hector'.

ISLAND ROOM

I am indebted to Ishbel MacKay for the true story, which became the central image of 'Island Room'.

AFTER

The Wannsee Conference decided on the implementation of 'the Final Solution'.

> Why should a dog, a horse, a rat, have life,
> And thou no breath at all?
>
> Lear, of Cordelia, in *King Lear* (Act V, Sc III) by William Shakespeare.

LEGACIES

The tenth ('I too remember holidays like that . . .') paraphrases WS Graham: 'Have the words ever/ made anything of you, near a kind/ Of truth you thought you were?/ Me neither.' from *What is The Language Using Us For*.

Seen/Unseen – in the card shop –
Congratulations on Passing your Dying Test